C000184996

Your Amazing I
Intuitive Hypno

15 Simple Steps to Seeing Inside the Unconscious Mind.

In this easy-to-follow Itty Bitty® Book, Saba Hocek guides you through skills that are attainable by anyone. This book is for both the beginner and experienced hypnotist and hypnotic subject, looking to explore new tools for a more impactful hypnosis experience.

Through these 15 steps, you will understand how to:

- tap into your intuition,

- learn a variety of methods and mediums to use your intuition,

- and apply these intuitive methods in hypnosis.

Pick up a copy of this valuable Itty Bitty® book to tap into this easy-to-use practice. Open yourself to new possibilities today!

Your Amazing Itty Bitty® Intuitive Hypnosis Book

15 Simple Steps to Seeing Inside the Unconscious Mind

Saba Hocek

Published by Itty Bitty® Publishing
A subsidiary of S & P Productions, Inc.

Printed in the United States of America

Itty Bitty® Publishing
311 Main Street, Suite D
El Segundo, CA 90245
(310) 640-8885

ISBN: 978-1-950326-65-5

To the spirits who have guided me and my husband, Bill, and son, Kenan, who have always supported me on my journey.

Stop by our Itty Bitty® website to find to interesting blog entries regarding hypnosis at:

www.IttyBittyPublishing.com

or visit Saba Hocek at

SelfEmpoweredMinds.com

Table of Contents

Introduction

You know what it means to be intuitive and you know what hypnosis is. But what is intuitive hypnosis?

Intuitive hypnosis is the method of using your intuition during hypnosis to get deeper into the unconscious mind and tap into the higher brain. This method allows you to go deeper, bypassing the conscious mind altogether.

In this Itty Bitty book, you will explore various methods and mediums to tap into the unconscious mind. Whether you are a professional hypnotist, hypnotic subject or one who indulges in self-hypnosis, you'll see how to use these methods and mediums.

You can supercharge your hypnotic experience by tapping into your intuition. As a self-explorer, mediator or hypnotic subject, you can double your outcome by enhancing your intuition. As a professional hypnotist, your sessions will be exponentially more powerful as you intuitively read your client's unconscious emotions and can then redirect your script to directly resonate with what you are reading in your client.

Everyone is Intuitive
Step 1
What is Intuition?

You are born with an intuitive mind—a third eye. How many times have you said, "I should have listened to my gut!" That was your intuition speaking! The more you ignore your intuition, the weaker it gets. Your intuition speaks through your thoughts, your dreams, and your visions.

To recharge your intuition:

1. Listen to your gut. Trust it and test it.
2. Write your dreams down. Was there a message? A warning? Reflect on the dream after a few days.
3. Look for "coincidences" and act on them. This is usually your intuition sending a message. Perhaps you see someone who looks like a friend, then call that friend.
4. When a random futuristic thought comes to mind such as an event that will take place in the future, write it down.

Naturally Increasing Your Intuition

The pineal gland—your third eye—is located in the center of your brain in direct line with the center of your forehead, about the size of a pea. It produces the hormones dopamine and serotonin, giving you motivation, awareness, and happiness.

To increase dopamine and serotonin:

- Avoid fluoride and processed sugar
- Take melatonin (not more than three months)
- Eat/drink beets or beet juice
- Take iodine supplements or eat iodine rich foods

Foods and herbs to strengthen the intuition:

- Anise – increases clairvoyance
- Bay leaf – stimulates psychic powers
- Lemon – increases psychic awareness
- Rose – enhances psychic powers
- Lavender – aligns the third eye
- Peppermint – heightens psychic awareness

Step 2
Accessing Your Higher Brain

Hypnosis is the state when you are between wakefulness and sleep. Hypnosis is the process of quieting the conscious mind so you can get to the unconscious mind and see, hear, and feel your limiting beliefs, negative thoughts, strengths, achievements, and potentials. In the hypnotic state, and when you have tuned into your intuition, you can access your super conscious state—your higher brain. It is there in your higher brain that you find:

1. Creativity
2. Inspiration
3. Brilliant ideas
4. Enhanced perception
5. Stronger confidence
6. Visions of the future
7. Insight into yourself and others

How Intuition Enhances Hypnosis

With self-hypnosis, you are toggling between conscious and unconscious states as you are bringing yourself into a state of deep relaxation. Your conscious mind often will interfere with the unconscious thoughts. However, when you are able to tap into your intuition:

- You can shut off the conscious arising thoughts more easily
- You're able to go deeper into the unconscious mind
- Your higher brain's thoughts are able to reframe the unconscious mind's limiting beliefs

As a hypnotist working with a client, tapping into the client's deeper feelings:

- Creates more easily a positive rapport with you and the client
- Brings awareness to the client more rapidly
- Allows the hypnotist to imbed the intuitive messages in to the script for a more effective experience

4

Step 3
Increasing Your Body's Vibration

Every cell in your body vibrates, and every emotion, every organ, everything has an optimal frequency. When you are vibrating optimally, then too is your intuition open and receptive.

To increase your vibration:

1. Rub your palms together for about 30 seconds creating friction.
2. Separate the palms so that they are barely touching. You should feel friction, a tingling feeling—your frequency. If not, repeat step 1.
3. Imagine there is a ping-pong ball between your palms, and you are rolling the ball in a circular motion keeping it in the center of your palms.
4. While feeling the frequency, increase the ping-pong ball size to a golf ball.
5. Continue to allow the ball to grow to a tennis ball, then a volleyball and perhaps even a basketball.
6. Now hover your hands over your face as though to be washing it.
7. Hover your hands over your forehead to stimulate your third eye.

Increasing Your Circulatory Vibration

The more oxygen to the brain, the more your intuition is stimulated. You can achieve this through:

- Exercise, such as brisk walks, jumping on a trampoline, or jumping rope.
- Abdominal breathing with yoga, meditation, or proper singing techniques
- Exposure to cold
- Music
- Binaural beats

The following breathing exercise quickly stimulates the third eye. Beware, as it can create a lightheaded feeling. Feel that your breath is coming from your lower back.

- Breathe in for 5 seconds; hold for 2 seconds and breathe out for 5 seconds.
- Immediately after, breathe in for 10, hold for 2, breathe out for 10.
- Immediately after, breathe in for 15, hold for 2, breathe out for 15.
- Feel the vibration in your mind and body. Anchor the feeling. It's important to recognize the sensation and commit it to memory.

Step 4
Open Your Third Eye

You have read about the incredible benefits when your third eye is open and the dietary intake or avoidances that enhance your intuition. Now, you will learn how to open your third eye using your own frequency. For best results, make sure to raise your vibration prior to these steps (see Step 3).

1. Place all five fingers of one hand very lightly on your third eye. This is located from the center of your forehead between your eyebrows.
2. Place the other hand's fingers very lightly on the nape of your neck where the neck meets the skull. Just hold your hands in place with your eyes closed.
3. Bring all your focus to the third eye.
4. You may experience warmth, or a tingling feeling on your third eye, or you may see colors or images. That is your third eye being stimulated.
5. Remain in that position for a few minutes.

Stimulating Awareness

Awareness is the key to a successful future.
Once you are aware of the intuitive signs, your
third eye can be readily accessed. Here you will
bring awareness to the sensations of a stimulated
pineal gland, your third eye.

- Hold your arms extended straight out to
  your sides, away from your body.
- With your arms still straight out to the
  side, bend your elbows so your palms are
  facing forward and fingers pointing up.
- Turn your palms in so they are facing
  your ears.
- Make a fist with both hands but leave
  only your pointer fingers pointing up.
- Holding your head straight ahead, look at
  both pointer fingers at the same time. If
  you cannot see both fingers, bring your
  arms in toward your center only as much
  as necessary to see both fingers
  simultaneously.
- Look at both fingers for 4 to 10 minutes.

Step 5
Seeing Auras

Auras are a field of energy surrounding a person. The aura has a color which is the expression of your physical and spiritual well-being. To first learn how to see auras, follow the steps below. Once you have done this several times, you'll be able to easily see the auras of others as well.

1. Get a white sheet of plain paper or locate a white wall.
2. Hold your left hand straight out in front of you using the paper or wall as the background.
3. Allow your fingers to spread comfortably apart and pointing up. For everyone, the left hand is believed to receive psychic energy.
4. Focus on the tip of your fingers and between your fingers
5. As you stare at your hand, notice a halo-like shape around your fingers.
6. Once you see the halo, wait to see its color. This may require patience.
7. Now that you see the color, you've seen your aura!

Aura Colors and Their Meanings

- RED is connected to the physical body, heart or circulation. It has the extreme emotions of anger, obsession, anxiety.
- ORANGE is connected to your reproductive organs. Physically it is associated with good health and vitality. Emotionally it relates to excitement, sociability, and productivity.
- YELLOW relates to spleen and life energy. It is the color of awakening, inspiration, and playfulness.
- GREEN is your heart and lungs relating to growth, expansion, and the healthy connection to nature.
- BLUE is associated with the throat and thyroid. Blue is the color of intuition as well as the love of others.
- PURPLE is the crown chakra, third eye and nervous system. This is everything you manifest. It is the higher intuition, the higher brain.
- WHITE is the ultimate connection of all, where you are one with the universe.
- BLACK signifies that there may be some negative energy that you are holding onto.

Step 6
Intuitive Colors

Just when you thought you understood all about colors, there's still more to know and understand. Recall the colors in your dreams or while meditating or during hypnosis. Your unconscious mind has chosen these colors for a reason and each holds a tremendous significance, giving you warnings, information, and insight into the future.

1. WHITE is clarity, wholeness, purity
2. GOLD is for wealth, prosperity
3. SILVER represents clairvoyance, personal transformation
4. PURPLE is about commitment and connecting with spiritual development
5. INDIGO is the sign of intuition, insight, imagination, and focus
6. BLUE is communication, creativity
7. TURQUOISE is healing, independence
8. GREEN represents love and forgiveness
9. YELLOW is generosity, confidence, ambition, courage, and inner power
10. ORANGE is sexual energy, happiness
11. RED represents survival, safety, family relationships, physical power, and vitality
12. PINK shows loyalty, warmth

Other Ways to Use Intuitive Colors

In this case, you are intentionally influencing your, or others', behavior through intuition colors.

- While meditating on yourself, a person or your hypnotic subject, influence a positive emotional state by seeing them engulfed in a color using the chart above.
- Wear the colors you wish to manifest, such as gold for financial abundance, or green for love. Now pay attention to events, coincidences, changes, or random acts throughout the day. Was it really just a coincidence?
- Wear the colors for the way you wish to feel or be treated. If you are experiencing any pain or ailment, wrap the area in turquoise color for healing. If you want to awaken your intuition, wear indigo, or to perform athletically better, wear red.
- Be aware of the colors in abundance around you. Are you suddenly noticing everyone wearing pink or yellow?

Step 7
Body Organs for Intuitive Hypnosis

Traditional Chinese medicine states that vessels run through the body, each leading to a major organ along which there are high energy points that get blocked from emotional, environmental, and chemical toxins. Through hypnosis you can release these stress blockages.

1. Take yourself or a hypnotic subject into a hypnotic state.
2. Ask the unconscious mind if there is any healing that is needed.
3. Scan your torso or have the subject scan their torso until tension, heaviness or stress is felt. Identify the organ by location.
4. Ask the hypnotic subject what color, texture, and energy it is holding.
5. Allow the subject to control the feeling by increasing that undesirable feeling, making the color, texture, energy more unwelcoming.
6. Now you can decrease that discomfort. Wrap the organ in a beautiful white light to reverse all negative energy, restoring vibrant color, soft texture, and energy.
7. Have the hypnotic subject scan their body and confirm that the pain, tension, or heaviness is eliminated.

Organs and the Emotional Connection

Each organ in your body has a function and emotional connection.

- LUNGS: depression, grief, sadness
- LARGE INTESTINES: holding onto the past, fear of letting go
- SMALL INTESTINES: feeling lost, abandoned
- STOMACH: anxiety, over thinking
- SPLEEN: mental sluggishness, dwelling on the past, worry, living through others
- HEART: sadness, depression
- BLADDER: fear of letting go, jealousy
- KIDNEY: indecision, discouragement
- GALLBLADDER: bitterness, lack of control, unfaithfulness, lack of courage
- LIVER: anger, irritability

Let's supercharge the hypnotic experience by releasing the emotional and physical blockages.

- Repeat processes 1-4 in Step 7.
- Identify the organ's emotion.
- Now ask the hypnotic subject to identify a past experience associated with the emotion that is linked to the organ.
- Allow the memory to be felt in the organ.
- Repeat 6-7 described in Step 7

Step 8
Skeletal Parts for Intuitive Hypnosis

Emotions are held not just in your mind or organs, but also in your bones. Before understanding the emotions associated with the bones, identify which skeletal part is holding the emotion.

1. Take yourself or hypnotic subject into a hypnotic state.
2. Ask the unconscious mind if there is any healing that is needed in the bones.
3. Scan your body or your subject's body for tension, pain or heaviness in the bones. Identify the skeletal part.
4. Ask the hypnotic subject what color, texture, and energy it is holding.
5. Have the hypnotic subject increase that undesirable feeling making the color, texture, energy more unwelcoming, demonstrating they are in control.
6. Now you can decrease that discomfort. Wrap the bone in a beautiful white light to reverse all negative energy restoring vibrant color, soft texture, and energy.
7. Have the hypnotic subject scan their body and confirm that the pain, tension, or heaviness is eliminated.

Skeletal Parts and Emotional Connection

Every part of your body has an emotional connection, and this includes the bones as well.

- Right side of body is partner (romantic/ business) or territory (home, office)
- Left side represents mother/child (switched for a left-handed person)
- NECK: flexible, willing, see possibilities
- ARMS: trusting to reach out to others
- HANDS: willingness to take
- HIPS: feeling supported
- LEGS: moving forward
- KNEES: courage
- FEET: having a goal, grounded

Every vertebra holds an emotion based on Louise Hay's work. Here are a few of the emotions:

- C1: Fear, confusion, running from life
- C4: Guilt, repressed anger, bitterness
- T2: Fear, pain, and hurt
- T5: Feeling stuck, rage
- L2: Stuck in childhood pain
- L5: Difficulty in communicating, anger
- Sacrum: loss of power

For a supercharged hypnotic experience, repeat for organs on page 14, as well as emotional connection with bones on page 16.

Step 9
Reading the Body

In the previous steps, you learned how to tap into your own body or instruct your hypnotic subject to tap into theirs recognizing the location where stress is expressing itself. In this step, you will learn how to read someone else's body.

1. Prior to hypnosis, stand a few inches to the left of your subject.
2. Ask the hypnotic subject to just be present and take a few deep breaths.
3. With your eyes closed, silently state, "I am a conduit here to receive from (person's name) any emotional or physical messages. Reveal to me, higher brain, through my body and only for this moment, what I need to know for their healing."
4. Starting from the top of your head, and moving slowly down, scan your body. Notice any tingling, temperature changes, pain, pulling, pushing, lifting, excitement or nervousness. It's very important here to really listen to the feeling.

Interpreting the Messages

In the previous steps you learned what each of the organs and skeletal parts represent and how to receive messages from your hypnotic subject's body. Now it's time to interpret them. Here is an example.

- Head:
  - Back of head: unable to let go of past
  - Above ears: obsessive thoughts
  - Forehead tension: difficulty focusing
  - Forehead stretching: having clarity
  - Tension around head: poor sleep
- Jaw: Tension, not expressing
- Shoulders: heavy, overwhelmed

Using the Messages through Hypnosis

Take your subject into hypnosis and supercharge their experience by:

- Adapting your script to include messages received, such as, "You are now ready to move forward. Notice how your feet are pointing forward ..."
- Ask your subject questions relating to the messages such as, "Imagine a tight band around your head ..."
- Ask your subject to feel the message such as, "I'd like you now to feel that sinking feeling in your gut ... Now feel it dropping out of your body ..."

18

Step 10
Turkish Coffee and Intuitive Hypnosis

Turkish coffee readings are an ancient tradition in Turkey used for intuitive readings. Each intuitive adds their own flavor to the method of reading. Below you will learn mine, Saba Hocek.

The small demitasse of Turkish coffee has a thick grind leaving a residue at the bottom of the cup. The following process prepares for the reading:

1. When drinking the coffee, hold the handle on the right.
2. When the last non-grainy sip is taken, place saucer on top of cup with saucer facing down and a little liquid left.
3. With thumbs on top and fingers on bottom make 3 rotations of the cup and saucer, right to left.
4. Flip the cup over towards your heart so saucer is now on the bottom.
5. Stand to the side of the person, read their body (see Step 9) while they rotate the cup in its saucer from left to right three times and they think what the cup is to reveal.
6. Let the cup and saucer sit for 15 minutes
7. It is now ready to be read.

Interpreting the Turkish Coffee Grinds

You've already gotten some information from your subject when you were reading their body. Use that information as you look at the cup.

- If the cup is stuck to the saucer, there's worry and heavy-heartedness.
- Starting from the handle, divide the cup into 4 even portions. Each section represents 3 months going clockwise.
- Generally, where there is clusters of coffee grinds, it is more negative while spots clear of the grinds is more positive.
- Look for images in the cup. Does the figure feel like your subject or someone else?
- Treat the cup as an artistic painting, interpreting the story.
- As you feel the stories being created in your mind, revisit what you have learned. Does it feel right in your body?
- Feel your subject's energy as you are looking in the cup.

You know how to read your subject's body and how to read their coffee grounds. You can now use this information during their hypnotic experience.

Step 11
Using a Pendulum for Intuitive Hypnosis

A pendulum is a weighted object suspended from a chain that swings freely back and forth. As an intuitive tool, a pendulum is an extension of your body through which your frequency is sent.

1. Always increase your vibration as described in Step 3.
2. Hold the pendulum very lightly with your thumb and pointer finger and without your elbow resting on a table.
3. With your eyes closed, ask the pendulum to show you *yes*.
4. Wait till you feel the pendulum swinging strongly before opening your eyes. Observe the direction it is swinging (side to side, front to back, clockwise, or counterclockwise). That is your direction for *yes*.
5. Repeat Step 4 asking to show *no*.
6. Repeat, asking to show *maybe*.
7. Repeat, asking to show *I don't know*. Now ask any question and wait for the pendulum to swing to get your answer. I suggest closing your eyes so you are not influencing the pendulum direction in any way.

Getting More Out of Your Pendulum

You can use your pendulum to ask questions about the hypnosis process. You can use your pendulum to answer questions beyond just yes and no.

- On a piece of paper, draw a circle
- Write several choices along the circle, spacing them evenly apart. For example, as a hypnotic choice, at 12 o'clock there could be "past life"; at 3:00 "future pacing"; at 6:00 "age regression", and at 9:00, "metaphor."
- With the pendulum in the circle center, ask a question. For the example given, ask, "Show the most effective method."
- With your eyes closed, wait until you feel the pendulum swinging strongly.
- Upon opening your eyes, you'll find it is swinging from the center to one of the written choices.

Another interesting and informative way to use the pendulum is to use another person's body. Hold the pendulum over an organ or chakra and see which way it swings:

- Clockwise: good energy
- Counterclockwise: restricted energy
- Front to back: partially restricted energy
- Side to side: energy out of balance
- No movement: no energy

Step 12
Using the Body Pendulum for Intuitive Hypnosis

You can also use your body or your hypnotic subject's body as a pendulum.

1. Stand very still, taking a few deep breaths. Note that as you get more experienced, you can do this sitting down as well.
2. Always increase your vibration as described in Step 3.
3. With your eyes closed, ask the subject to show you yes.
4. Observe the direction you or your subject is moving, (side to side, front to back, clockwise, or counterclockwise). That is the subject's direction for *yes*.
5. Repeat Step 4, asking to show *no*.
6. Repeat, asking to show *maybe*.
7. Repeat, asking to show *I don't know*.
8. Now ask any question and see in which direction you or your subject is moving to get your answer.

Applying the Body Pendulum in Hypnosis

Now that you know how to use your body as a pendulum to ask questions about the hypnotic subject, you can supercharge your hypnosis sessions by knowing the answers from their unconscious mind.

- As you work with your subject, notice the subtle movement in their body. For example, when you say, "You are now ready, even eager, to move forward..." observe the sway of their body. Is it in the direction of yes?
- Ask yourself a question about your subject, such as which method would give the most ingrained results, or is the issue related to a childhood wound.
- Listen to your mind and body applying what you learned in earlier steps about colors, organs, skeletal parts, and reading the body.
- Combining all of the above, you will give your hypnotic subject an amazing session!

Step 13

Using the Body Dial for Intuitive Hypnosis

This particular method is a combination of reading the body and pendulum work. It is an extremely powerful method, as it is so effective and foolproof.

1. Imagine a dial in the center of your chest
2. At the 6:00 point it's zero (0); at 9:00 it's 25; at 12:00 it's 50; at 3:00 it's 75 and again at 6:00 it's 100.
3. Ask yourself or your hypnotic subject a question.
4. Ever so slowly, begin to turn the dial in your minds eye from zero toward one hundred.
5. As soon as you feel resistance, stop.
6. Where the dial stops is your answer. The numbers indicate the percentage. For example, if the question were, "Should I change jobs?" and the dial stopped at 50, then the answer would indicate that you should change jobs, but there's more to consider since it is only at the 50 marker.

Digging Deeper for Answers

The body dial allows you to dig deeper, like peeling away at an onion, to get to the core of the problem or answer.

- If after asking the body dial you get less than 100, then you will want to dig deeper.
- You can then ask questions such as, "Is there something I can do to change the outcome?" or, "Is there something in my past that needs healing?"
- Each time, as you investigate further, ask "with this change, will I ...?"
- Continue until you reach one hundred, where you have the final answer!

Remember to apply all the intuitive techniques from previous steps to supercharge your hypnotic experience.

Step 14
Inner Voice Intuitive Hypnosis

The more your third eye is opened, the easier these methods get. Once you are intuitively confident, you begin to hear the answers.

1. Initially, it is best to use an object as a tool to focus. While holding the pendulum, have it swing from side to side and follow it with your eyes.
2. Ask a question, and then quietly listen for the answer.
3. Pay attention and respect when the inner voice commands you.
4. Always thank the inner voice for providing answers.

Turn Up the Volume

To increase the volume of your inner voice:

- Increase your vibration (step 3)
- Meditate, especially in the mornings, for 10 minutes or more
- In a silent space, repeat your question several times, then wait for the answer
- Write your question on a piece of paper and place it under your pillow before sleeping.

Step 15
Nailing the Power

You've learned so many wonderful ways to tap into your intuition—your higher brain—where you can sense right down to the cellular level of the mind and body. You also learned various hypnotic methods to use with the intuitive knowledge. Here is the final step allowing you to experience, or allowing your client to experience, a supercharged intuitive hypnosis session.

1. Experiment, experiment, experiment! You will want to experiment with each of the methods described throughout this book.
2. Perform with confidence and conviction.
3. Feel self-assured to modify or implement your own nuances. Make it yours!
4. Most important, FEEL. Whether you are performing self-hypnosis or working with a client, the key to success is to fill your heart with compassion and to listen, feel, hear, and be there in that moment.
5. Notice bodily sensations confirming your intuition such as a rush of goose bumps after stating a prediction.

Looking to the Past to Change the Future

Throughout this book you have learned to apply intuitive methods while being present to influence or interpret your, or your subject's, future. Now you will learn to see the past life of the subject.

- Increase your vibration (step 3)
- Focus on the back, base of your head
- Feel it opening up
- See a light shining in
- Now, in your mind's eye, imagine turning your face around so that you are looking into the base of your skull
- Remain in that state quietly giving full focus and attention
- Listen for any messages, notice any images, feel any body sensations.

Using all the knowledge gained from this book, you can now understand the past life of the subject paving their road to Live Life Empowered!

Now that you have seen how to ignite your intuition and super charge your hypnosis processes, discover how to activate your inner genius to Live Life Empowered!
https://selfempoweredminds.com/genius-activator

You've finished. Before you go . . .

Tweet/share that you finished this book.

Please star rate this book.

Reviews are solid gold to writers. Please take a few minutes to give us some itty-bitty feedback.

ABOUT THE AUTHOR

Saba Hocek, a professional healer, holds six certifications, accredited by BANHS and is a member of the Association for Transpersonal Psychology & Hypnotherapy. At a young age she recognized her intuitive healing gift though she went on to become a software applications developer.

Fresh out of college, Saba developed the first PC based reading system for the blind and visually impaired. Within just a few years, her company, Adhoc Systems, became the leader in that industry.

Saba Hocek's extensive software and systems development work with the mental health industry led her to realize the connection between the flow of computer logic and the human mind giving her an insight into healing that few people have. Her fascination for the brain, curiosity of her intuition and desire to foster the inner power of others, drew her to become certified in Hypnosis, EMDR and Access Consciousness as well as a Certified Specialist in Biofeedback and Certified Brain Coach for Amen Clinics. Self Empowered Minds offers modalities of hypnosis, biofeedback, reiki and intuitive readings enabling people to **Live Life Empowered!**

If you enjoyed this Itty Bitty® book
you might also like...

- **Your Amazing Itty Bitty® Meditation Book** – Rhona Jordan

- **Your Amazing Itty Bitty® Physic Abilities Book** – Craig Junjulas

- **Your Amazing Itty Bitty® Body Life Connection Book** – Suzy Prudden and Joan Meijer

And our many other Itty Bitty books available on line at www.ittybittypublishing.com.

Printed in Great Britain
by Amazon

79076346R00031